Leading Without the Title

A Blueprint to Growing into Leadership

Wendy Norfleet, Ph.D.

Visit me at NorfleetSolutions.com

ISBN: 978-1-7356304-0-3

Library of Congress Control Number: 2020916284

First Edition
Printed in the United States of America

Cover Designed by Jeane Sumner, Website HQ

Disclaimer

This book is designed to provide information and guidance to its readers and to serve as a supplement to career coaching/mentoring and professional development training.

DEDICATION

To my husband Al, and our daughters, Camille and Summer, for allowing me to disappear and write. I hope I did you proud.

CONTENTS

ACKNOWLEDGEMENTS

I want to thank God for being with me when I did not think I could finish this book.

I want to thank all my clients that gave me such positive reviews and feedback.

I want to thank Mia Alexander and Rosalind Downer for their constant encouragement.

.

INTRODUCTION

"Ambition is the first step to success. The second step is action."
Unknown

Many have heard some variation of the Peter Principle. The Peter Principle says that people get promoted to the level of their incompetence. In fact, you probably know a person or two that fits this saying. Thank goodness that you may also know people that obtain promotions and do a fantastic job in their new positions. People fitting the Peter Principle may have received the promotion based on current skills, but once promoted, the skill sets needed change. The people that do well are those that have good foundational leadership skills, flexibility, adaptability, and in essence are true change agents.

This book is very dear to me as it contains information that I wish I had when starting my career. Instead, I learned many of these lessons through trial and error. Luckily, you will not have to do the same. I created this book as a blueprint for those who are looking to lead an inspiring life and further develop their leadership skills. With a strong foundation of basic leadership skills, you will find yourself with the ability to successfully adapt to each situation you face.

When I am asked to speak on leadership, I often have to respond with an inquiry as to what aspect of leadership should I address. Obviously, leadership is too broad a topic to adequately cover in an hour or two. After working my way up to executive-level leadership and years of speaking on this topic, I have decided to take my experience and create a series on leadership. This first book will help you speed up your path to success, whether you're just beginning your career journey, working toward a leadership position or simply want to be better positioned for promotion. Remember, leader does not have to be in your title for you to display leadership characteristics.

To help you better develop the leader in you, this book will focus on a couple of key topics to place you on the right path as you climb the career ladder. The areas covered are:

- Self-Leadership
- Understanding People
- Communication
- Finding Your Tribe
- Know Your Personal Return on Investment (PROI)
- Appreciation and Recognition

1: SELF-LEADERSHIP

"Mastering others is strength. Mastering yourself is true power."
Lao Tzu

Along my career journey, I often meet those that have aspiration to join the ranks of leadership. Equally important, I also meet those that do not want leadership roles, but still have the desire to put themselves on a rising career trajectory. Whether you are seeking a leadership role or simply positioning yourself for promotion, you will need to utilize many of the characteristics often identified as leadership characteristics. Over and over again, it has been seen that demonstrating your leadership traits is a great way to get promoted or hired for a new job, no matter which type of role you're going after.

Self-leadership Defined

In my last workshop for those entering the information technology field, I worked with a diverse group of individuals that had one thing in common: they were all looking to succeed. Although some had aspirations for leadership and others did not, it was soon evident that helping them identify the leader in themselves would pose a wide array of benefits. After receiving several questions about how to position themselves for leadership, I emphasized the fact that you cannot lead others until you know how to lead yourself.

In one of its definitions, self-leadership is defined as:

- Being self-aware

- Ability to set your goals

- Honoring yourself

- Rejecting pessimism

- Being a change agent

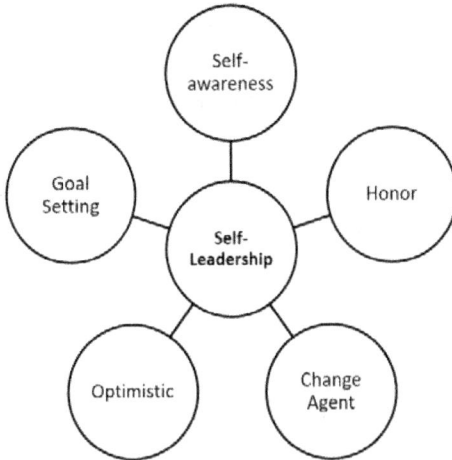

Self-leadership is about choosing who we are, what we do and who we become. It is not permission to apply a selfish approach to get what you want at any cost. Rather, it's about being intentional and acting with purpose. The path to self-leadership is seldom easy, but there are a few mindset changes that will make the path much easier.

The world, with its reliance on technology and interdependent economies, has become a place that leverages knowledge. Because of this, the things we learn can become obsolete very quickly. What remains constant is that we have to manage ourselves effectively within these complexities and ongoing evolution to overcome obstacles, to renew and refresh ourselves and to fully participate in our lives.

Although self-leaders can make great managers, self-leadership is not about managing others. Rather, the focus is about leading yourself.

In a typical look at external leadership, a manager gives

directions, sets expectations, and tells you when something is due. They may ask how you would like to get the work done, but they still define what the end result will be. A self-leader scans their own environment, recognizes what they can do, and then takes action to produce the desired outcome. In talking about self-leadership, Peter Drucker states that self-leadership is being the CEO of your life.

Foundational Questions

To be successful at self-leadership, there are foundational questions that should be addressed. These questions focus on better understanding oneself.

Self-Leadership Foundation Questions	Who Are You?	Identify what is important to you and what you believe in.
	What Do You Do?	Identify your behaviors, motivations and goals.
	What Do You Need to Learn?	Identify gaps in knowledge and setting up a learning plan.
	How Do You Use What's Available?	Implement habits for success.

Who Are You?

Answering the question, "Who Are You?" can be done in a variety of ways. While most people can easily provide answers, many of those answers end up being glib responses that don't accurately reflect who you are. This answer requires the ability to identify what you believe in, your core values and what's most important to you.

As it turns out, it doesn't take years of self-reflection to uncover your core values. In the Appendix, I've provided a quick 10-minute exercise to help you figure out how you're showing up in your personal and professional life. Once you complete this exercise and identify what's important to you, you'll be able to get closer to your goals and live your truth by acting in alignment with your values.

Obviously, introspection can vary from person to person and should not be taken lightly. Once you self-reflect and identify your core values, you'll be able to bring your most authentic self to the table, radiating in any space you enter, just like a true leader. I can recall one of my high school teachers just brimming with energy that drew people towards her. I was impressed, influenced and motivated by her. While, I did not want to be her, she helped me realize that when people know who they are and find a career where they can bring their authentic self to the table, they ignite the spirit of those around them with their passion.

What Do You Do? What Do You Want to Do?

Now that you have, in essence, identified who you are and what you value, your actions must be aligned with what you want to achieve. Living out your core values is the most fulfilling way to succeed. Most of us have heard some variation of the quote, "Action speaks louder than words." This is where the rubber meets the road. Here, you can dream and envision your future all you want, but you must be able use those behaviors and motivations to capture a plan that allows you to reach your goals. Keep in mind that although you will make plans, plans are living documents and should be reviewed and adjusted periodically. The path to success is never smooth or predictable, and we must adjust accordingly. That being said, there are an infinite amount of actions you can take that align with your core values. Staying true to your purpose throughout the ups and downs will allow you to reach your goals and live out your vision of success.

Hopefully, you will use your values as guidance in establishing these goals. Goal setting should take place on multiple levels. I began each day with a daily goal (to-do) list, but I also have longer term goals that will allow me to achieve my personal vision.

Personal
Vision

2 – 3 Year
Goals

Monthly Goals

Daily Goals

When I coach clients, they often bring a variety of goals that they want to work on. After speaking with some of them, I realize that we often have to back up and do a couple of exercises that allow me to better understand them. When you take the time to understand what is important to you, you are better able to set goals and perform actions that are aligned with your core values.

Some questions to help your self-discovery and to jumpstart the process of setting goals are:

- What would I do if there were no restrictions?

- What can I do to achieve that goal?

- What are known obstacles?

- Are the obstacles real or perceived?

- What can I do to overcome these obstacles?

Initially your goals may be vague and lack enough information to make them attainable. The more specific the goal, the more clarity you'll have on your way to achievement. Make sure you are setting Specific, Measurable, Achievable, Realistic, and Timed (SMART) goals. When setting goals, other than your daily to-do list, make sure you can address each of the components of setting SMART goals.

It's crucial to view your goal from a variety of angles. Life does not stop just because you have decided to work toward your goals. One way to ensure you address the many possible barriers is to take a comprehensive view of what you want to achieve and its relationship to what is going on in your life. The image below will help you assess your potential obstacles and plan a path to success in accordance with your daily life.

Commitments
- What other commitments do you have?

Timeline
- What is a realistic timeline with milestones?

Opportunities
- What changes can I take advantage of?

Resources
- What resources are available that will assist'in achieving my goals?

Threats
- What will prevent me from reaching my goals?

The more you know about yourself, the better you will be at documenting meaningful goals. That being said, there are often things we need to work on before moving forward. After all, we won't be able to identify what's meaningful until we understand the values that lie within us. I often recommend to my coaching clients to perform a personal strengths, weaknesses, opportunities and threats (SWOT) analysis to better understand themselves. Once you gain a deeper understanding of who you are and what you value, you'll be able to eliminate the non-essentials and focus on what's more meaningful to you. Below is a template that I use with many of my clients when setting their goals.

Goal Setting Template			
	Strategic Actions (to move you toward your goal)	Beg Date	End Date
Goal 1:	1.		
	2.		
Resources:	3.		
	Strategic Actions (to move you toward your goal)	Beg Date	End Date
Goal 2:	1.		
	2.		
Resources:	3.		

What Do You Need to Learn?

Don't assume that because you now know what's important to you and you've written some goals down that you're done. Making this assumption implies that you are armed with all the knowledge that you will need. If this were true, you would already be in the position that you wanted. Sometimes we get so full of ourselves that we become our biggest roadblock, creating self-imposed limitations by underestimating our need for change or improvement.

Even if you are fortunate enough to have the initial knowledge needed for your quest, there will be additional learning needed along the way. As you may have already figured out, many of our career choices prove that learning does not stop when we leave school or embark on a new endeavor. With rapid technological advances, our large network of global relationships, the desire to keep abreast of global economies, and the ability to learn and continue to seek knowledge are all essential aspects of life today.

Lifelong learning is a significant part of self-leadership and demands a commitment of self-leaders to continually seek knowledge.

How Do You Use What's Available?

While achieving your goals takes time and patience, there are things that you can do right away that will improve your chances for success. I am sure that, like me, you have read or been given numerous lists of habits for successful people. When I first started my career, I admit that I was somewhat overwhelmed by all the recommended actions on these lists. Thankfully, while extensive, the habits that you select for implementation are completely up to you. Whether you adopt one or multiple habits, this action is an opportunity to make improvements using techniques that have proven to be successful for others. Be careful making your selection, as not only should they improve your career, but your well-being. In fact, the two often go hand in hand. Remember that if you do not take care of your physical and emotional health, you cannot support the demands you are making on it with our career pursuits.

In my research, I found that the seven most common habits for success are:

1. Meditate

While the meditation form may vary from person to person, the benefits of meditation are plentiful and includes reducing stress and increasing self-awareness.

2. Stay the Course

Things will not always be easy, but realizing that and being prepared to stay the course is an essential habit for those seeking success.

3. Eat Healthy

In today's fast-paced society, it is becoming more common to skip meals or make unhealthy food selections. It is our responsibility to take care of our body by eating healthy.

4. Exercise

Regular exercise has enormous, medically-backed benefits. It has been found that people who exercise live longer and healthier lives. Exercising regularly may mean a walk twice a week for some and a daily run for others. You determine what exercise looks like for you.

5. Share with Others

Successful people demonstrate their generosity through the willingness to share their knowledge or skills. This is also a form of giving back and is greatly appreciated. Since successful people often reach their goals with the help of others, they're often eager to share their knowledge with those who are in the same place they used to be.

6. Say No

This was a very necessary, but very hard habit for me to adopt. I had to realize that it was okay to say no. Most of us are extremely busy with a lot of stuff going on. We cannot possibly say yes to everything. If we did, we'd find ourselves too busy to complete our own tasks. Once you get to know yourself better and identify what's important to you, saying no will allow you to focus on your goals and speed up your path to success.

7. Set Big Goals

Don't let anyone limit your vision. Be intentional about what you want your future to look like. Dream big. You'll make the necessary adjustments to your activities to work toward your goals. While you may have to change the path to reaching your goals, never reduce the size of the end goal—that's a self-imposed limitation.

Ultimately, success is never random, and successful people often have key habits in common. Implementing these habits into your daily routine will help you stay motivated, maintain your emotional and physical well-being and arm you with the ability to say no to things that do not align with your vision of success. Once you're able to eliminate the non-essentials and only engage in things that bring you closer to success, both your career and life will become more fulfilling.

2: UNDERSTANDING PEOPLE

"Any fool can criticize, condemn and complain but it takes character and self-control to be understanding."

Dale Carnegie

Many people would say that they understand others, but when pressed to explain how, they have no answer. To make sure we are on the same page, let's start with gaining a better understanding of others.

We have all probably heard the phrase – "Men are from Mars and Women are from Venus". There is more to understanding people than simply knowing what planet they are from. Let's start our journey together by providing a definition of what it means to understand someone.

How Do I Understand People?

Understanding someone means to have the ability to empathize with that person, being able to think along the lines of what the other person is thinking and being able to reason out what transpired in their mind. That's a lot to do, but it is not as difficult as you may think. Empathy lies in the foundation of better understanding others. Think about it. What are some ways we can better understand others? I can give you a long list, but I found that if you focus on three particular things, it will carry you far in understanding others.

1. **Recognize that we are all different.**

    If we were all the same, we would all have the potential to be experts in understanding people. However, that is not the case. People have different personality types and different motivations. We must also be cognizant that even after identifying a person's personality type, motivations, experiences, situations, culture, race, and even a person's current mood can all influence behavior.

2. **Keep an open mind.**

    Avoid assumptions, appreciate differences and practice empathy. We probably all know someone in our lives that if we had not kept an open mind they would not be in our inner circle of friends and acquaintances. I can recall when I first moved to Jacksonville, one of my administrative assistants sent out an e-mail message to the entire team. It started off with "…it is with chagrin that I inform you of the passing of …." I was so upset. Why was my assistant writing that it was with humiliation and embarrassment that we were being informed? Not only was I upset about the message, several off my staff had stopped by the office to express their displeasure in the notification. I headed over to talk with her and because I had already had other things I was displeased with and did not want to bring those things up, I decided to ask her a question instead of reprimanding her. When I asked her why she sent the message out, she said she wanted everyone to know of the passing. I then asked why she was embarrassed to inform the staff of the passing. She said she did not know what I meant. I had her look up the definition of chagrin and I could see her embarrassment. It turns out that English was not her first language and, in her culture, chagrin is another word for melancholy, which means saddened and heavy-hearted. Believe it or not, that exchange changed our relationship. It brought home the realization that to understand people, you must keep an open mind.

3. Understand yourself.

Explore your personality. Understanding yourself, even on a basic level, is helpful. Keep in mind, you can't lead others until you're able to lead yourself. There are so many assessments available to better understand your biases and stereotyping. We all have them. When people learn that I like country music, they often do a double take. If they take the time to dig deeper, they realize that I like most music with the exception of hard rock. You should also know, in regard to yourself, that there may be times that no matter how well we listen to others and empathize, we are just not going to understand them. However, we can still accept them.

Even armed with this information, please do not think that you will ever know all there is to understanding people. No matter how much I learn, I realize that there is still much I do not understand. Each day, I continue to try my best. I have noticed that while I may not completely understand people, somewhere along the way, I have become pretty good at it and this understanding helped me develop influence.

What Does Influence Mean?
John Maxwell states that everyone has influence. Some of you may recall Dale Carnegie's book, How to Win Friends and Influence People. This book provided five methods to become a person of influence:

- Show genuine interest in someone else

- Remember people's names

- Listen

- Make others feel important

- Smile

Influence is often equated to power, but it's much more than that. Influence is crucial because it represents an emotional connection to people. Further, it is often believed that true influence involves building trust.

No matter who you are, where you work, or what your professional goals are, achieving more influence in the workplace can put you on the path to success. Gaining influence on a team can help you work together more effectively. Gaining influence in a supervisory position can make you more respected, more appreciated and can help your team more readily align their views to yours. Gaining influence in a meeting can make your voice more likely to be heard and acknowledged.

Influence has countless advantages, but gaining that influence, like learning a skill, takes time and effort. Fortunately, there are many strategies you can use to cultivate this characteristic.

1. Build Trust with Your Co-Workers

   Influence is most often and most easily carried through trust. Only when a co-worker trusts you will he or she be open to your influence. If you're in a higher position in the company hierarchy, it's possible to convey a demand or assign a task that must be carried out by your employee, but true influence suggests a free will component.

2. Cultivate Reliability Through Consistency

If you execute your tasks efficiently and on time, day after day, people will eventually come to rely on you. You are letting your leadership characteristics shine through by allowing your team, manager and employer to see you demonstrate consistent results with your good work. Consistency is vital for building influence because it proves that you're reliable, making people more open and trustworthy of your decisions.

3. Be Assertive, Not Aggressive

Being assertive is the only way to get your ideas noticed, especially when you're competing with others for visibility, such as in a meeting. However, there's a difference between being assertive and being aggressive. Assertiveness should extend as a general quality to all your interactions, regardless of whether you're speaking to colleagues above, below, or at your level, and regardless of the conversational format. Being assertive, so long as you truly believe in what you're saying, is a way to cultivate a reputation of authority and earn the ability to influence your peers and employer.

4. Be Flexible

While this may seem like it conflicts with the need to be assertive, being too stringent or adamant, and not being open to the possibility of changing your opinion, will work against you. People will come to see you as stubborn, and having a reputation as being stubborn will decrease the respect people have for you, compromising your overall influence. While being assertive means you have confidence in your beliefs, flexibility means you're also open to new and innovative ideas. Once others know that you're open to their suggestions and altering your beliefs when needed, they'll be more confident and comfortable while communicating with you.

5. Be Personal

When trying to build influence in the workplace, a little personality goes a long way. If people can't sense that you're being authentic, they won't be as open to your influence or ideas. Being personal is especially important as you're climbing up the career ladder. If you isolate yourself, or try to build your perceived authority by distancing yourself from others, it might only serve to alienate you and put you in a position where you're viewed with distrust, resentment or "not a team player". Influence can never be achieved in isolation, since you need to have significant impact on others to be an influential figure.

6.   Focus on Actions Rather than Words

Trying to build influence through words is useless. Each time your actions fail to match up to your words decreases the meaning of those words. We have all known someone that can recite at will all the wonderful things they have done. However, if pressed, no one can remember any actions that supported this recitation. People won't remember what you say, they'll remember what you did and how it impacted them. If you're going to build influence in the workplace, you need to speak through your actions, or, at the very least, have the actions and history to back up whatever you're saying. This proves your reliability and ability to follow through.

7.   Listen to Others

Influence is a two-way street. The more you believe in the people around you and incorporate their ideas into your vision, the more they'll believe in your ideas and incorporate them into their work habits. If you want to build up this kind of relationship with your co-workers, you first have to listen. Take time to respect and acknowledge everybody's opinion and let people know that you value them. Valuing a person can be something as simple as respecting a person enough to listen to what they are saying, even if you disagree. As you can see, understanding people and influencing people go hand-in-hand.

Webster dictionary defines influence as the act or power of producing an effect without apparent exertion of force or direct exercise of command. As you notice, influence can be the catalyst of action without direct command. As opposed to ordering others around and exerting a power dynamic, creating equally beneficial and empathetic relationship is one of the most effective ways to urge others to act. Start building your influence by understanding others and making these types of connections.

3: COMMUNICATION

"Communication is a skill that you can learn. It's like riding a bicycle or typing. If you're willing to work at it, you can rapidly improve the quality of every part of your life."

Brian Tracy

Have you ever wondered why it seems so difficult to talk with some people, yet so easy to talk with others? Is this a result of our poor communication skills or theirs? Actually, neither choice is correct. Communication is much more complicated than we realize. In this chapter, we'll explore the communication process, the impact of communication skills and how we can utilize cues to better communicate.

What Is Said vs. What is Heard

Words, throughout any medium, are the most powerful building blocks of communication. Our words are what provide meaning. Throughout our lives, we can positively challenge ourselves by learning new and improved ways of communication. In fact, particular words can drastically enhance our communication with others.

What we say is not always what the other person hears. Our message goes through a complicated system of filters and outside influences before it reaches the recipient. This is why it is important to follow-up on our communication messages and ensure that mutual understanding is reached.

The Communication Process

To better understand the importance of communication, we can say that good communication is like having a conversation. Most of us want to do our part in a conversation and realize that it takes effort to get results. A meaningful conversation involves actively listening, putting aside our assumptions, and working toward a shared meaning or understanding through the exchange of the conversation. In a conversation, we participate as part of the social norm. Have you noticed that when we are in a conversation, we do not usually have debates or employ tactics to try to change someone's opinion? Instead, we want to make sure the receiver understands our message as it was intended. Keep in mind that all communication takes place with both the sender and receiver's biases.

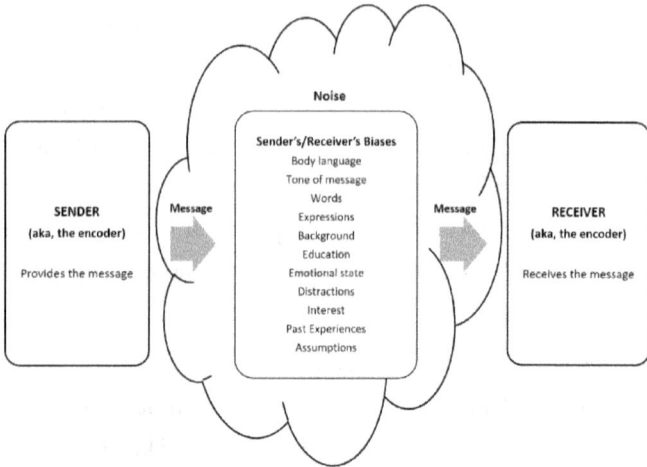

There is more behind the communication process than simply sending and receiving messages. In today's society, most of us lead busy, complicated and fast-paced lives. Additionally, our messages are provided through many modalities – text, email, memo, social media, etc. As such, we may send messages after thoughtful consideration or on the fly by sending a quick text or e-mail message. Our messages are encased in a shroud of noise. This noise is representative of our perceptions, what is being communicated, our environment and of course our biases. Yes, we all have biases. Our biases are not always negative, but they do impact our ability to communicate on both ends of the message. We are all guilty of having taken something said the wrong way.

Some communication mistakes are common and recognizing that they frequently occur, steps can be taken to prevent them. The top five items to check when communicating are:

1. Edit Your Communication

    Take the time to check your message's spelling, tone, and grammar. Making these mistakes can make you appear unprofessional and careless.

2. Respond, Not React

    Responding is usually done by thinking your point through and calmly sending your message. Reacting is when our emotions are driving and messages are sent without thought. Reacting instead of responding can damage your reputation and give others the impression that you lack self-control.

3. Verify Message is Understood

    Take the time to check if the receiver of your message has understood your communication. This verification should be sought regardless of the message modality.

While no magic formula exists to overcome this communication noise, there are many techniques we can use to ensure that our communication is as clear as possible. Since communication often starts with the message, a good rule of thumb is to practice creating clear, concise and compelling messages. Ensure that you are communicating so others can hear.

Listening

Listening is often considered one of the foundations of communication. As we previously discussed, listening and hearing are not the same thing. Most of us were fortunate enough to be born with hearing, but listening is a skill that must be learned and practiced. When you hear something, sound enters your eardrum, passes through your ear canal, and registers in your brain. Listening is what you do with that sound and how you interpret it once it registers.

Here are some tips for successful listening:

- Listen intentionally.

- Listen to understand.

- Listen with interest.

- Get rid of your assumptions.

- Listen for what is not said.

Listening is hard work. When other people are listening to us, they have the same difficulties we do in trying to focus on the message. Our minds wander, noises or thoughts distract us and we can be thinking about what to do or say next.

Practicing active listening means that we try to understand things from the speaker's point of view. It includes letting the speaker know that we are listening and that we have understood what was said. Active listening can be described as an attitude that leads to listening for shared understanding. Instead of listening to respond, active listeners listen to understand.

When we make a decision to listen for total meaning, we listen for the content of what is being said as well as the attitude behind it. Is the speaker happy, angry, excited, sad... or something else entirely?

The communication message is one thing, but the way that people feel is what gives full value to the message. It's important to read between the lines and listen for what is not being said. Responding to the speaker's feelings adds an extra dimension to listening. Are they disgusted and angry or in love and excited? Perhaps they are ambivalent! These are all feelings that you can respond to in your part of the conversation. This will make the entire dialogue more meaningful and prove that you're actively engaged.

Message Cues

In addition to the written or spoken message, the communicator often provides addition cues that help us better understand the message. Active listening means that we are also very conscious of the non-verbal aspects and other auditory sounds. Other questions to consider are:

- What are the speaker's facial expressions, hand gestures, and posture telling us?

- Is the speaker's tone loud or unsure and hesitant?

- Are they stressing particular points?

- Are they mumbling or having difficulty finding the words to express themselves?

Listening Cues

When you are listening to someone, there are techniques to apply that demonstrate you are paying attention to the speaker, provided you are genuine in using them.

Physical indicators include making eye contact, nodding your head from time to time and leaning into the conversation. You can also give verbal cues or use phrases such as "Uh-huh," "Go on," "Really!" and, "Then what?" Another technique is to use questions for clarification or summarizing statements. A few examples are:

- "Do you mean they charged you $7 for just a cup of coffee?"

- "So, after you got a cab, got to the store and found the right sales clerk, what happened then?"

Tips for Better Listening

- Make a decision to listen. Close your mind to

clutter and noise and look at the person speaking with you. Give them your undivided attention.

- Do not interrupt people. Make it a habit to let them finish what they are saying. Respect that they have thoughts they are processing and speaking about, and wait to ask questions or make comments until they have finished.

- Keep your eyes focused on the speaker and your ears tuned in to their voice. Do not let your eyes wander around the room, just in case your attention does too.

- Carry a notebook or start a conversation file on your computer. Write down all the discussions that you have in a day. Capture the subject, who spoke more (were you listening or doing a lot of the talking?), what you learned in the discussion, as well as the who, what, when, where, why, and how aspects of it. Once you have conducted this exercise eight to 10 times, you will be able to determine the level of your listening skills.

- Ask a few questions throughout the conversation. When you ask, people will know that you are listening to them, and that you are interested in what they have to say. Your ability to summarize and paraphrase will also demonstrate that you heard them.

- When you demonstrate good listening skills, they tend to be infectious. If you want people to communicate well with you, you must set a good example.

Creating Positive Relationships

One winning communication strategy is to lead with the goal of developing a positive relationship with others. Most of us want to do well in life and work, but on a smaller scale, we want to look forward to our day. Who wants to get out of bed feeling apprehensive toward those we must communicate with? Creating positive relationships is key to making both yourself and others happier at work and in life.

Communication Strategies for Stronger Relationships

These 10 tips to build stronger, positive relationships can be utilized by everyone.

1. **Smile at people.** It takes almost 4 times as many muscles to frown as it does to smile.

2. **Speak to people.** It is always nice to receive a cheerful greeting.

3. **Learn people names.** Most people welcome hearing their name used properly and positively.

4. **Be friendly and helpful.** Think of the adage, show yourself friendly. When you open yourself up, you will gain friends.

5. **Display positivity.** Speak and act with a positive attitude. Positivity is contagious.

6. **Show interest in people.** You can find things to like in almost anybody if you're looking.

7. **Be generous with praise.** What are you saving it for?

8. **Show consideration.** Assume good intent.

9. **Provide service.** There are numerous opportunities to give service. Many of our most meaningful moments is what we do for others

10. **Have a positive sense of humor.** Have a positive sense of humor – Ensure humor is not achieved at the expense of others.

None of these tips are rocket science, but our ability to apply them sometimes slip away from us unless they are ingrained.

4: FINDING YOUR TRIBE

"People inspire you, or they drain you. Pick them wisely."

Les Brown

Relationship building is a key component for career success. Often, careers are built outside of the office. So, how do we build meaningful relationships rather than just a large collection of business cards or transactional connections?

Networking

Despite being a key skill in building a successful career, many people are not networking. So, how do you develop new and existing contacts? Remember, you may have a lot of contacts, but these are not automatically relationships. Networking is defined as interaction with others to exchange information and develop professional or social contacts. Networking goes beyond collecting business cards and a single meeting. Effective networking involves building a strong well-connected network of relationships.

For many people, attending a networking event causes great paralysis. Networking often gets a bad reputation as a place where fast-talking people are looking to shake hands, tell you what they do and pass out as many business cards as possible. But in reality, whether we do it well or not so well, we network every day. We do it with family, friends, colleagues, clients and acquaintances.

At its most basic form, networking is forming and building relationships. If you only take (or sell), your network will be weak. If you mainly help and give, your network will be strong. Always approach networking with the hopes of providing value to others. Give before you take or ask.

To many, this may seem counter-intuitive, but it works. I think we are all familiar with the adage that anything worthwhile is worth working for. I may not be quoting it exactly right, but you get the point. So, another way to look at networking is that a good network is created and successfully maintained by the application of hard work. A network without the work produces nothing worthwhile. Building a network isn't about how many contacts you have saved or business cards you have collected, it's about how many meaningful relationships you have throughout a particular industry (or various industries).

A relationship is defined as the way in which two or more concepts, objects, or people are connected, or the state of being connected. As human beings, we are social and want to feel connected. Can you image living in Jacksonville, where the population is approximately 900,000 and feeling no connection to anyone? It would be pretty lonely. I think that is what drives us to make initial connections and in turn cultivate those connections into relationships.

Relationship building has now become an essential skill. With the necessity to building relationships both locally and globally in today's workplace, you should focus your attention on answering these questions:

- What is the best way to form relationships?

- How can I make the most of my network?

- What type of relationship do I need?

How to Network

Identify and target connections that are relevant to your goals, industry, interests and/or skill set. Relevance can be according to such things as location, social grouping, industry, and gender. The more relevant your targeting of groups, the easier it will be to build relationships. Direct your efforts beyond obvious business people and obvious networking groups, but be mindful of the nature of the group and conduct yourself appropriately.

The clearer you've identified your career goals, the easier the path to get there. The same goes for networking. The more specific your networking goals, the better the results when networking to reach your goals. When deciding who to network with or which events to attend, be sure to evaluate your upcoming career goals. Ask yourself which milestones you're trying to reach and how you'll get there. Consider connecting with others whose work you admire and those who have completed projects that mirror your next career goal.

Once you've identified a particular group of people to network with, make sure you're aware of the group's needs, expectations, rules (official and unofficial), and membership composition (formal or entirely random), and adapt your style and methods accordingly.

Certain non-business professional people can be hugely influential in networks, and greatly trusted because of their neutrality and professional standing – educators, scientists, journalists, magistrates, and politicians, for example. It is not easy to make connections with these people through conventional business networking, but remember that a network is not only made up of business people, and may be open to these non-commercial connections.

Within most networks, people tend to have a few close and trusted connections. Choose these, your most trusted and closest associates, very carefully.

Reputations are built according to your chosen contacts, in addition to how you yourself behave. The old expression is generally true: "You can tell a woman or man by the company she/he keeps." Focus your efforts on groups and connections of integrity, as well as relevance. You can identify your target group criteria in your networking strategy or plan.

Building Lasting Relationships

Never underestimate the power of connections. One fleeting connection can be built into a long-lasting relationship that turns out to be vital. Whether in terms of your life or career, each connection you make can mean all the difference. After all, who is doing today what they did 20 years ago? These relationships that we build are not just about securing opportunities, but inspiring others, exchanging ideas, and collaborating.

Developing successful professional relationships creates a welcoming environment where people are inspired to reach their maximum potential. Thus, developing successful relationships requires leadership skills and strategies.

The core factor that drives successful relationships is making people feel important. One can do this by paying attention to people and using common courtesy. For example, greeting people and asking how they are doing, shows a sense of care and acknowledges their presence. Another way to acknowledge that people are important is showing appreciation. This can be done by simply saying "thank you." Another way is leaving a "thank you" note for individuals who have helped you. Always give credit for contributions, never take credit for something others have done even if you were leading the project or task. Showing appreciation lets people know that they are important and that they contributed to the success of your work.

When networking we are often building towards long-lasting relationships and should keep in mind that as with growing anything, relationships are developed through nurturing. Sustaining authentic relationships through networking is often achieved by:

Being Open

Be open to meeting new and different people. When I first moved to Florida, I was looking to meet people to build up my social and professional connections. I have found that I am a better person when my circle extends to different people, including ethnicity, background, experiences and thoughts. How can you grow if you only associate with people just like you? The best way to expand your mindset and worldview is to communicate with those who you wouldn't have otherwise.

Being Discerning

With today's technology, it's never been easier to connect. However, I think most of us acknowledge that if we connect with a couple hundred people per week, not all of those connections will evolve into meaningful relationships or into members of our tribe. One way to potentially have more meaningful relationships is to be intentional on whom we choose to build relationships with. I was talking with a colleague and we were discussing the circle of trust. This term refers to a concept that while we may have many acquaintances, we are particular choosing who to build relationships with and finding our tribe or circle of trust.

Keeping It Real

While many of us appreciate a good newsletter, this form of communication cannot replace a well-written or texted message conveying authenticity with no ulterior motives. Don't shoot the messenger! I realize that many connections are made to eventually do business. However, it has been proven that taking the time to build a relationship provides abundant benefits as people are more likely to interact and do business with people they know.

Many studies have shown that customers are over 30% more likely to buy from a brand that aligns with their core values. Similarly, the more you act in accordance with your values and connect with those who support this mission, the easier it will be to turn those connections into meaningful relationships. Even further, being intentional about the way you network will allow you to gain influence and build a tribe that aligns with your purpose.

Following Up

Have you ever attended an event and met a couple of professionals that you really enjoyed talking with and promised that you would follow-up, but didn't? Many of us have been guilty of this. Now using LinkedIn on my cell phone, my follow-up has become almost instantaneous. When I meet someone that I want to stay in contact with I send them a brief note to connect in LinkedIn, stating where we met or why I want to connect. Thankfully, with these reminder cues in the message, I have not had anyone not connect with me.

Following up is just as important as making the initial

connection. The new business cards in your pocket will never manifest themselves into meaningful relationships until you master the skill of following up. Only then will you be able to collaborate, expand your network, and exchange ideas with other like-minded professionals.

The networking balancing act will be to continue cultivating current connections, while making new ones. Yes, it can be challenging, but if you create a plan that works for you, you truly can accomplish both activities.

Finding Your Tribe

Finding your tribe differs from networking. While we hope that our networking eventually develops into meaningful relationships, whether personal or professional, your tribe usually reflects your values and becomes your community, giving you a sense of belonging. If you find networking difficult, finding your tribe may be even more arduous. However, while more difficult to find, our tribe is easier to recognize as it is usually instinctive.

Over the course of our lives, we are part of many tribes - from family, sports, affinity groups, workplace, and many more populations. We are social beings and have a need to belong. Have you noticed that we have a tendency to gather and commune in familiar groups? We find our tribe by seeking those with shared interests and passions. Our tribe is elevated in importance as it reflects our values as well as fulfilling our need to belong. Most of us seeking authentic connections from our tribe, realizing that this may require effort, authenticity and vulnerability on our part.

The quest for your tribe is very personal. We are all different in what we seek and there is no single plan that can be provided. However, there are some suggestion that may ease your search for your tribe.

Self-reflection

What type of community do you need? Identify what area do you want more support or development. Maybe for you, you are simply seeking like-minded people.

Try Something New

Remove your preconceived notions. Often we avoid certain individuals or groups because we feel they are too different or they may not want to include us.

Volunteer

When volunteering for a cause you are passion about, you will likely find others with the same passion.

Sign-up for a Class

Have you always wanted to learn something? Meeting a person in a class can provide a safe atmosphere to get to know others.

Create Your Tribe

With today's wide use of social media and Meet Up groups, you can put out a call to attract the type of people you want in your tribe.

Similar to networking and paving a path toward success, finding your tribe is all about living in alignment with your values. Connecting with those who have shared interests and passions will allow us to expand our reach. The more people you communicate with, the bigger your network. That being said, it's crucial to be selective about finding your tribe.

Being part of a group is more about quality and less about quantity. Having 10 friends that share similar values to you is more impactful than having 50 random acquaintances. It's only when we connect with those who support us, and vice versa, that we can live in authenticity and identify our tribe.

5: KNOW YOUR PERSONAL ROI

"An investment is deemed an investment only through its returns."
Lamine Pearlheart

When I discuss leadership and its characteristics, the conversation often turns to how you present yourself to others, particularly, how we quantify our experiences or value to our current or potential employer.

About ten years ago, I was one on the shortlist of candidates for a president position. I had previously worked with the company and had achieved many major accomplishments when working with them. I felt pretty good going into the interview with the selection committee. After entering the room and going through the introductions, I was told that as this was the first round of interviews, each candidate would be limited to approximately 30 minutes. When I was given this time restriction, I felt that I had to provide succinct answers to the questions asked to ensure that I did not run over my allotted time. Unfortunately, at the end of the interview, I was not feeling as confident as when I started. While I felt that I answered each question, something was missing. A few after sending a thank you note, I reached out to the Chief Human Resource Officer (CHRO). I was honest and said that while I thought I was a great fit, I did not feel that I would be advanced to the finalist position and if true, would it be possible to meet so that I could get feedback on the interview. After the finalists was selected, we met and I was told that if I had added the details (told the story) behind my achievements, I would have been one of the finalists. This information truly supported that the details matter and started my search for how best to support my value.

ROI vs. PROI

Most people understand the concept of return on investment (ROI). It is usually explained as a performance measure and evaluates the efficiency of an investment. The ROI is a ratio between the cost of an investment and its net profit. A high ROI means the investment is favorable to its cost.

Personal return on investment (PROI) is a term that is being heard more frequently. There is not a lot of difference between ROI and PROI as they both refer to a profit realized from a resource minus the original, or ongoing, investment. So, what's the big deal? PROI is ROI applied to human capital. And yes, the employees are the human capital. When PROI is discussed, it refers to how you, the employee, are substantiating the company's investment. With company resources for investment often being limited, the reality is that if you ignore identifying your value to your employer, it is at your own peril.

While some employees voice disparaging remarks against employers, organizations are in fact allocating resources and salary for each position. What many current or potential employers would like answered is, "What are you doing for me? To answer this question, you should be answering this inquiry by identifying what distinguishes you from your peers, documenting what you are really good at and providing substantiated statements on what makes you worth your company's investment. In other words, how do you personally help the company achieve its corporate goals?

No matter your title or where you are on the corporate organizational chart, you must provide value and be able to demonstrate that value by answering the organization's question of what's in it for me. Adequately answering this question is often done in the form of telling a story. And no, it is not a long-winded rambling story.

Telling Your Story

I mention telling your story, because presenting your value must always be done by providing the context. I shared with you my personal story and while I answered all the questions, I failed to put the answers in context and that was the missing component.

When working with one of my clients and helping them to identify their value, all accomplishments were bulleted. As we reviewed them, there was one that stated, "Achieved a $250,000 profit." While this may be considered a great achievement, when I started asking questions to find out the context, there was story to be told. Working with her team for approximately 14 months, my client was able to turn around two cost centers that had carried more than an half-million deficit and showed a profit in both cost centers totaling a little more than a quarter of a million dollars. By telling her story, a current or future organization learns that my client is a good leader, works well with a team, is good with responsibility, knows about working with budgets, and has perseverance. There are a few other traits that are provided, but I think you get the point. Without the context, her value may have appeared underwhelming.

You may often think that people know your accomplishments or what you bring to the table. Don't make the assumption that when it's time to deliver promotions or reductions that your actions are in the forefront of their minds. Documenting your accomplishments through stories will make those activities more memorable, and focus on the process along with the outcome. Taking a look at the PROI cycle demonstrates the importance of being able to quantify your accomplishments. We see that what matters is measured, what is measured get done, what gets done gets rewarded and what gets rewarded matters. It is an ever-revolving cycle.

```
What gets  ➤➤  What
rewarded       counts get
counts         measured

    ⬆   PROI CYCLE   ⬇

What get    ◀◀  What gets
done gets       measured
rewarded        gets done
```

You may be wondering how to add metrics to your accomplishments. I admit, this is easier with sales positions and those positions that have built in metrics, such as production work. However, while not exact, it is often possible to convert your value into a monetary amount, which is universally understood.

When working with a client whose position is a retention specialist, we were able to do some research on what it takes to obtain a new client versus retaining a client in that industry. Using these figures, we were able to identify how much my client was saving the organization. Another example closer to home may be when you were asked to be over two positions due to someone transitioning. Knowing the ballpark salary of that second position and taking into account how long you hold both positions, you would be able to quantify your savings to the organization. While it may take some effort, being able to tell your story is an ability that each person must master. Lots of people can do what you've done, but you're the only person who can do it your way.

6: APPRECIATION AND RECOGNITION

Recognition is not a scarce resource. You can't use it up or run out of it."

Susan M. Heathfield

My goal here is to make sure that the importance of appreciation and recognition is understood. According to multiple studies on why employees leave their places of employment, not being appreciated shows up in the top ten of each study and more often than not in the top five. Knowing the importance of this, let's take a look at how you can demonstrate positive recognition and celebrate success.

Recognizing Others

You may be wondering if your attention to recognition will have an impact on your colleagues or team members. Rest assured; your authentic recognition does carry weight. Thankfully, not all forms of recognition have costs. It costs nothing but a moment's time to stop at a colleague's desk to say, "Good job on that report" or "Thank you for adding your expertise". In fact, due to our new COVID-19 normal, colleague recognition is even more important with the increased remote workers and virtual teams. Making this special effort to recognize colleagues become even more important as they may feel separated from the workplace culture and camaraderie due to their geographical separation.

Most of us have people in the workplace that we gravitate toward, but to provide meaningful recognition, it should be fairly distributed. If work or service is recognition worthy, then it should be recognized regardless of who performed the action. Consistency in recognition is important for it to be valued. If you recognize only one colleague when three performed the action being recognized, you show favoritism for one colleague, while disregarding the work of others.

One of the easiest ways to build relationships is through recognition. In some instances, it is easy to identify when someone has gone above and beyond, such as a co-worker offering to help you meet deadlines on your project. In other situations, you want to ensure your recognition is appropriate. Recognizing a colleague for the minimum job expectations serves no true value and in fact, can cause a colleague to stop striving for performance success. Instead of rewarding the bare minimum, recognizing others' hard work and praising them for going above and beyond will let them know that you appreciate their efforts, improving the trust and communication in the relationship.

Delivering Recognition

One of the great aspects of recognizing and celebrating colleagues is that you do not have to wait for a special day or designated holiday. There are a variety of ways in which the recognition and celebration can be done. Prior to management, I celebrated my colleagues' assistance on projects I was assigned with a handwritten note. I was able to purchase a dozen note cards for just a few dollars, costing about twenty-five cents a note. Because I took the time to hand write the notes and they were personal to each co-worker, they were greatly appreciated and allowed me to express my appreciation. Additional ways to recognize colleagues are:

Social Media Shout Out

Using social media is a great way to recognize a colleague. Before using this method of recognition, make sure your colleague is not averse to public recognition.

Say Thank You in Public

This can be done in a team or company meeting. Allows you to share your appreciation in front of others.

Private Message

A great and personal way to recognize a colleague is to privately call or message them.

A Card or Gift

This may be used for more celebratory occasions, but it's a great way to let them know that you're celebrating their most recent success. It's also a creative and personal way to show appreciation.

APPENDIX: VALUES EXERCISE

As I mentioned, it does not take years to uncover your core values. This is a simple exercise that jumpstart the process of identifying your core values and start the process of aligning them with your personal goals. This exercise should not take more than 10 minutes to complete. Ready, set, let's go!

The table below has 84 core values. Feed free to add any values that you feel are missing.

Accountability	Accuracy	Achievement
Altruism	Ambition	Assertiveness
Autonomy	Balance	Being the best
Belonging	Boldness	Calmness
Challenge	Cheerfulness	Clear-mindedness
Commitment	Community	Compassion
Competitiveness	Consistency	Contribution
Cooperation	Correctness	Creativity
Curiosity	Determination	Devoutness
Diligence	Discipline	Diversity
Economy	Effectiveness	Elegance
Empathy	Enjoyment	Enthusiasm
Equality	Excellence	Expertise
Exploration	Expressiveness	Fairness
Faith	Family	Focus

Freedom	Fun	Generosity
Goodness	Grace	Growth
Hard work	Happiness	Harmony
Health	Honesty	Humility
Initiative	Independence	Insightfulness
Intelligence	Intuition	Joy
Justice	Leadership	Legacy
Mastery	Make a difference	Openness
Originality	Peace	Popularity
Power	Prosperity	Respect
Risk-taking	Safety	Self-control
Self-reliance	Simplicity	Sincerity
Spirituality	Stability	Strength
Stewardship	Structure	Success
Support	Teamwork	Thoughtfulness
Timeliness	Trustworthiness	Truth-seeking
Understanding	Uniqueness	Unity
Usefulness	Vision	Vitality

1. Identify Your Core Values

From the list of core values, choose each core value that resonates with you. Selection should be made by emotion, rather than overthinking each word. As you read through the list circle or write down each word that feels like personal core value for you. Don't forget if you feel a core value you possess or resonates with you is missing, write it down.

2. Group Similar Values

Take a look at the values that you have selected and group them in a way that makes sense for you; creating no more than a maximum of five groupings. If you create more than five droppings, review and drop the least important groupings until you have no more than five. See the example below.

Fun	Balance	Growth	Fairness	Ambition
Enjoyment	Calmness	Hard work	Equality	Challenge
Happiness		Diligence	Unity	Success
Joy			Belonging	

3. Choose One Word from Each Group

Select one word from each group that best represents the label for the entire group. Remember, this is part of identifying the best value for you. In the example below, each of the selected words are bolded.

Fun	**Balance**	**Growth**	Fairness	Ambition
Enjoyment	Calmness	Hard work	Equality	Challenge
Happiness		Diligence	Unity	**Success**
Joy			Belonging	
			Harmony	

4. Add Action to Each Value

Add an active very to each value. This allows you to view each core value as actionable. See examples below:

- Seek joy.
- Live in harmony.
- Pursue success.
- Embrace balance.
- Pursue opportunities for growth.

As I mentioned, one of the most important things you can do for yourself is to identify your core values. A well-lived and purpose-filled life is achieved when living a life aligned with your core values.

NOTES

Dale Carnegie & Associates., & Cole, B. (2011). How to win friends and influence people in the digital age. New York; Toronto: Simon & Schuster.

Drucker, P.F., "Peter F. Drucker on self-leadership," in IEEE Engineering Management Review, vol. 34, no. 2, pp. 17-17, Second Quarter 2006.

Gray, J., (1992). Men are from Mars, women are from Venus: a practical guide for improving communication and getting what you want in your relationships. New York, NY: HarperCollins.

Peter, L.J., & Hull, R. (1969). The Peter principle. Morrow.

ABOUT THE AUTHOR

Dr. Wendy Norfleet carries a long list of industry certifications, which includes John Maxwell Leadership Certification, Life Coach Certification, Lean Six Sigma, and numerous awards for service and leadership. She is the CEO and founder for Norfleet Integration Integrated Solutions (NIS) and leads a team of highly qualified professionals that work with individuals and corporations to provide strategic training and coaching solutions. Dr. Norfleet's strengths are her extensive leadership experience, strong IT background, determination, and creativity. She thrives on challenges, particularly those that benefit her clients.

Dr. Norfleet practices what she preaches. She serves on several boards, is a member of Leadership Jacksonville, volunteers for several community organizations, and is a long-time mentor for Take Stock in Children. One of her favorite things to do is to help others be successful.